MAKING WATERCOLOR
BEHAVE

"THE BRIDGE AT RONDA"

Awarded the Irving Brokaw Prize at the combined exhibition
of the American Water Color Society and New York Water
Color Club, 1930.

Making Watercolor Behave

WITH TWO REPRODUCTIONS OF PAINTINGS
AND TWENTY-ONE PHOTOGRAPHS
DEMONSTRATING BRUSH WORK

BY ELIOT O'HARA

New York

MINTON, BALCH & COMPANY

1932

Printed in the United States of America

CONTENTS

ILLUSTRATIONS

7

8 ILLUSTRATIONS

INTRODUCTION

THIS book, written primarily for beginners in watercolor, may be of equal service to the student or amateur, who, having done some drawing and painting in oils, wishes to develop a technique for watercolor work. His object in experimenting with watercolor may be to make this popular medium his chief form of expression; or he may want to use water for gathering color notes or material to be used later in producing oils. Many painters in oil derive their pictures from quick watercolors, some of them the merest indications of a color relationship, or a record of a fleeting moment which would have been lost while an oil palette was being set. When the note or a rough sketch is made, it is quickly dry and packed, brushes are clean and one is ready to move on. Speed of getting an effect, quickness of drying, light weight, cleanness and permanence make this medium an ideal one for either the amateur or professional on a vacation or voyage.

Contrary to the usual belief in America, watercolors are just as permanent as oils. This is understood in England where they have been used since the time of Turner in a proportion only recently equaled in this country. How many painters of only a few years ago are to be known to posterity, if at all, by their watercolors rather than their oils! Sargent, for instance, in the last generation, I suppose, thought of his oils as his most important works and the watercolors and drawings as mere relaxation. The oils are discoloring and cracking and the watercolors, except where unreliable colors were used, are not changing. Henri's oils as well show the ravages of a relatively short time. It is a pity he did not do more watercolors.

The chemistry of oil paints is rather complex. Intimate mixtures of different oils, pigments, varnishes, dryers and thinners all go in together, sometimes even over unfixed charcoal drawings or tempera (watercolor). These divers mixtures vary even with the same painter as he has a whim for this or that material. When an oil is to be corrected or worked over, new layers of hardening mixtures are superimposed or a paint remover is added to the forces of destruction. Watercolor, on the other hand, is simple. If something is to be corrected, a new coating of paint will rarely do the job so that an entirely new sheet of paper must be used. The only things involved are paper (a good linen paper will not perceptibly fade or change color), a single medium and pigments. Of course, water will loosen the paint and if the picture is not covered with a glass, finger marks and extraneous dirt which cannot be removed with an eraser will damage it. In justice to oils, however, it should be said that if they are properly applied and the right combinations of pigments are used,—as for example, in the flesh tones of Velasquez,—they will remain almost unchanged for centuries.

Since the time of Leonardo, painters have had the notion that along with their genius for portrayal, for interpretation, or for presenting abstraction, must go excellence in the chemistry of paints. The earliest painters had to make their own, and a sorry job they did of it for the most part. Why should recent painters stew up messes of secret varnishes or grind colors in competition with modern chemists? If painters ever had money to lose, such experimenters would be like the business man who, having made money in manufacturing, spends his last years losing it again in financing other industries. "He even grinds his own paints" nowadays is not as complimentary a remark as it used to be.

To paint good watercolors is a full time job, not a relaxation from other kinds of artistic expression. It can be an extremely difficult medium to work in if one is to utilize all the different techniques and procedures, and strive for the utmost variety in modes of expression. A mastery of all the methods and a ready command of a specific treatment to suit a mood, time of day, climate, temperature, or whatever one wants to express, are prerequisites for the professional watercolorist; that is, the one who does only watercolors, not watercolors, portraits, oil landscapes, and etchings. Many painters can do adequate work in more than one of the allied arts. Indeed, in most cases a moderate amount of experimenting in all of them will help any single line, and they should all be worked at by every student in order that he may find out which gives the most satisfaction.

The choice of subject matter, or outer stimuli which one looks at or feels in order to draw (mental raw material for pictures), should, unlike the choice of a medium, be kept as flexible as possible unless one wishes to become a specialist. Specialists in subject matter often become famous and often make money. It is a fine thing to be known as a good painter of nymphs, boats, snow scenes, abstractions of guitars, or any other one specialty; but the danger is that such a painter suffers from without through people saying he cannot do anything else, and from within through the effect on his ingenuity and imagination; with the result that his pictures get more and more like each other as to time of day, color and feeling. It is for the individual painter to choose whether he wishes to specialize or not. I find that I relish most the exhibitions of painters in whose work something unexpected—either good or bad—can happen.

In writing on the technique of watercolor painting, I shall try to avoid other subjects such as color harmonies, composition and the philosophy of art, except as they intrude themselves.

It is possible to teach a technique or method for using brushes and paint. Facility is a tool with which the student should be provided. As to what he expresses with the tool, that is his own affair. He may, if he chooses, study with a master, but should be careful not to imitate the master. He can learn rules and formulae for composition which his teachers have found successful, and thus make composition according to whatever set of conventions are in fashion at that school. But he will probably learn as much in breaking the rules as in following them, and perhaps produce as good pictures.

In color he can be taught that certain colors are pleasing together. Matisse, or some other colorist, has found the different combinations and they are there to be used, but what of it? There are just as many more good ones to be found and if the artist has good taste, he will find them; if not, his color will be either imitation or bad.

The best training for walking alone is walking alone. I might be able to tell what I know about composition or color, but in more senses than one it would not do the student much good. If, however, I can teach him how to do the mechanical part of producing a watercolor, such as: tinting a paper, blending colors, or performing the various other operations or tricks of the trade; then if he has anything to express, his hand will be ready. In other words, I shall try to give him the spelling and grammar;—he must have the ideas.

MAKING WATERCOLOR
BEHAVE

MAKING WATERCOLOR BEHAVE

CHAPTER I

THE SIMPLEST TECHNIQUE

MANY who have tried to do watercolors have given up too easily. Frequently their discouragement at not making the colors go where they want results merely from the use of some unsuitable material.

Certain methods and materials are easier for the beginner to start with. I shall describe the simplest only, leaving the more difficult to take the form of notes or amendments relative to experiments with other papers and materials which can be tried later.

Leaving aside for the moment the use of opaque watercolor and dealing with what is usually known as pure watercolor,—that is the use of white paper and semi-transparent pigments for light colors instead of a mixture with opaque white,—there are four major techniques.

Methods

1. *The English method* consists of superimposing light washes of various colors over each other, letting them dry between each coat. This is the technique usually described in books on watercolor.

2. *The "sewing-up" method* consists of using a rather wet brush but leaving white paper rims between the brush strokes to prevent their running together into pools. If a hard edge is wanted between two strokes it is filled in *after* both strokes are dry; if a passage or blending is wanted the drying is timed until either a partial or complete blending will result from joining the strokes.

3. *The smooth paper method* necessitates care in preventing the colors from running together when they should be distinct, and in allowing them to run together when blending is desirable. Subtle differences in value and tone are accomplished in this blending which are difficult to control but extremely effective when they are successful.

4. *The dry brush method,* except for large areas or washes, requires the use of so little water in the brush that accidentals and run-ins become of less importance. This method is more deliberate and leaves less to chance than any of the others except

opaque painting. For this reason we will call it the simplest method.

There is no hard and fast dividing line between these four classifications and they are more often than not used in combination.

David Cox and the earlier watercolorists generally used the first method. The work of George Pearse Ennis illustrates what can be done with the second. Charles Woodbury's watercolors are largely on smooth paper. John Whorf often uses a dry brush. These names are given so that the student may identify the four methods. The excellence of the painters mentioned is, of course, not due to method; and no doubt each has at some time used all the methods either in turn or in combination.

Materials for the Easiest Technique

Paper. Heaviest grade of rough paper in block form, any size between 10 x 13 to 14 x 18. Canson and Whatman have proper qualities for this trial. If possible, get it thick enough so that the detached sheets can be used back as well as front, because we are to use up a lot of paper. (Other papers and their purposes will be taken up later.)

Box. Most boxes are too small—get the largest size of japanned metal box with depressions or partitions for squeezing out tube colors. Buy an empty box and supply colors and brushes of your own choosing.

Water Bottle. Container for water should have a screw top and wide neck and be somewhere near the size of a drinking glass. A mayonnaise bottle is good.

Colors. Tubes, not pans. Any manufacturer— Newman, Weber, Winsor Newton, Devoe, Horadam—to mention a few. For the coal tar colors, Schmincke, Talens, or Eilida. (Colors are more thoroughly dealt with later.)

A good set for study of summer landscape would be: alizarin crimson, French ultramarine blue, cobalt violet deep, Antwerp blue, lemon yellow, aureolin, cadmium yellow medium; cadmium orange, orange vermilion, burnt sienna, sepia, raw umber, ivory black and Davy's gray. And of the coal tar colors: brilliant turquoise no. II, yellow green no. I, and brilliant orange no. I. Aureolin and the cadmium colors are expensive; one could use chrome yellows which are not so permanent.

Brushes. Sign painter's lettering brush, flat, ¾ inch wide, ox-hair. This brush has the advantage of being capable of any width stroke from its maximum width to a pencil edge, according to whether

I

After the pencil lines roughly indicate the areas to be filled with color, the area with the lightest value is painted in.
The brush is 1 inch wide; the paper, 15 x 20 inches.

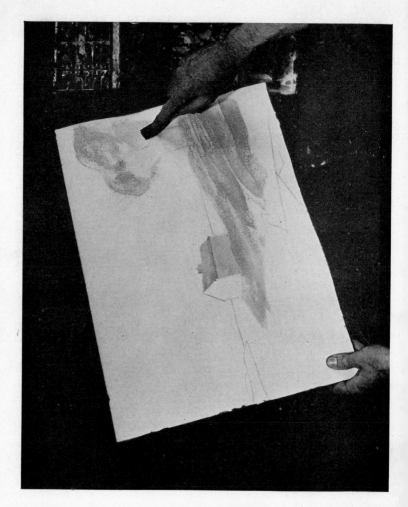

II

A brush-stroke with the forefinger pressing on the bristles of a dryish flat brush makes broken color on rough paper.

it is moved sideways, diagonally or edgewise. Grumbacher makes good ones; but art stores carry many varieties. This brush can do most of the work; but, in order to achieve fine lines and necessary detail, a medium-sized watercolor brush, round, and coming to a sharp point when wet, or a line brush, which is round, thin and with all the hairs the same length, may be substituted.

Miscellaneous. A square of cheese cloth or cotton, art gum, a pencil (medium hard), a low camp stool.

Procedure

In painting watercolors, it is convenient to draw rough pencil outlines of the main areas of color, at first, at any rate until the control of the brush becomes through habit partly subconscious. Number in pencil the color areas in the order of their value (lightness or darkness), starting with the lightest as number one; for this is the order in which we shall paint them. Suppose that the picture has been sketched in single pencil lines showing, for instance, the horizon, the outlines of a house or boat, or the trunk and top edge of a tree. Then one is ready to start the color.

Wet oil paint will stick to a vertical surface, but watercolor will run and drip unless the pad of paper is horizontal. I find that the best way is to sit on a child's folding camp stool 6 to 8 inches high with the pad between one's feet. By leaning slightly forward one lets the right arm swing naturally over the paper from the shoulder and move in any direction without effort and without unnecessary muscular tension. This position has another advantage, which is, that by placing one's back to the sun, one casts one's own shadow on the paper and need not look for other shade. The paper should not be in the sunlight during work except possibly during waits for drying.

If the pad can be placed on a slightly rounded bump on the ground or a folded coat, it is kept from collecting dust at the wet edges and also it can be tilted, rotated or turned upside down with the left hand. This is convenient because the right hand can draw a truer line from left to right than in any other direction. In doing a thin mast, for instance, the paper can be turned on its side.

With the pad between the feet, the paint box and bottle of water can be at one's right. A very low horizontal platform or table might serve to raise the pad to a level less back-breaking than that of the ground.

Before starting, the necessary colors should be

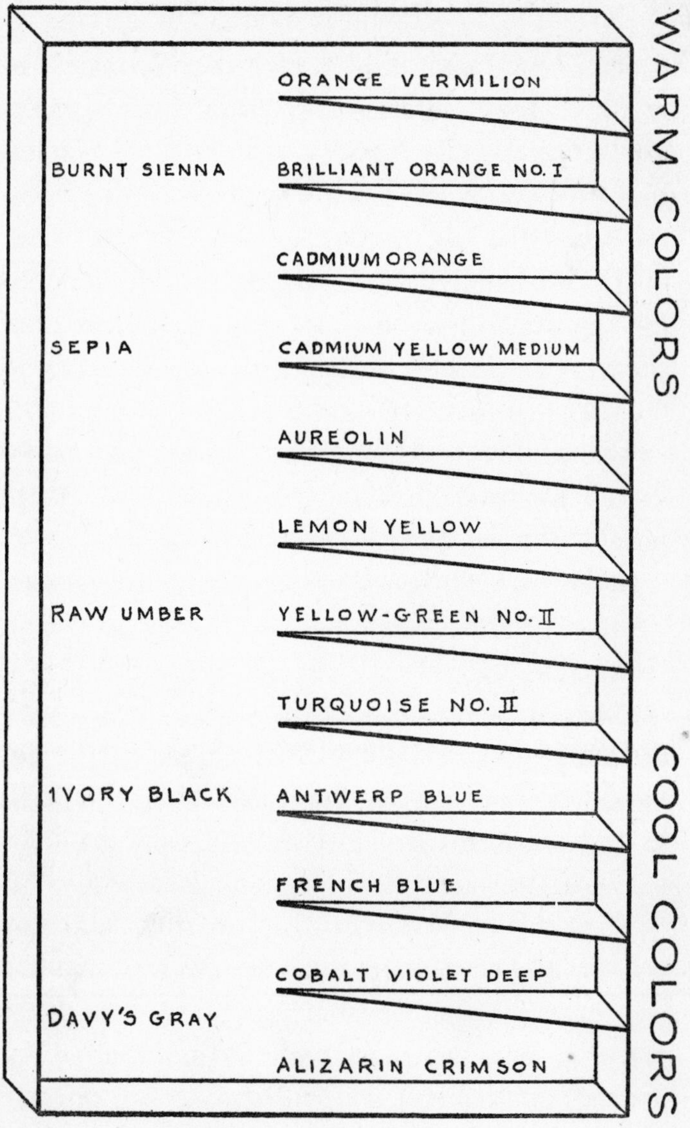

WARM COLORS

ORANGE VERMILION

BURNT SIENNA   BRILLIANT ORANGE NO. I

CADMIUM ORANGE

SEPIA   CADMIUM YELLOW MEDIUM

AUREOLIN

LEMON YELLOW

RAW UMBER   YELLOW-GREEN NO. II

TURQUOISE NO. II

IVORY BLACK   ANTWERP BLUE

FRENCH BLUE

COBALT VIOLET DEEP

DAVY'S GRAY

ALIZARIN CRIMSON

COOL COLORS

squeezed out into the depressions in the box. I like to keep them in the order of the spectrum with the bright colors on the top and the darker ones below.

It will be seen that the above division of the spectrum between the warm and the cold reds, brings all the warm colors together on one side and all the cold colors together on the other. If one wants a bright color, one takes it pure from anywhere on the top row or mixes pigments which lie next to each other as one combines alizarin crimson, and French blue for purple. To obtain a dull color, one either chooses it from the lower row, or uses a dull color to modify a bright one.

Finally, being ready to put on color, the first thing is to decide which color is the lightest; because, while dark colors can be put over light ones in watercolor, it is difficult to put light colors over dark. There is no need of wetting the paper as a preliminary. If a yellowish house in sunlight is the lightest value in the picture, put that in first. To do this, dip the large brush in water and give it a shake, that will give you about the right amount of moisture, then touch it lightly to the desired yellow or orange in the box and fill in the outline, keeping the pad level so that the color will not run. If you find the value is too dark, rinse the brush and flood in a little water, then squeeze the moisture out of the brush by passing it between the thumb and finger of the left hand, or, wiping it with a cloth, soak up the water from the paper. The brush when dry and clean will take off water or paint while it is still wet as well as put it on. If the color is not reddish enough on one part of the house, add a little red while it is still wet and let it run together. It is better to mix two colors this way right on the paper than to mix them in the brush or the box. You should work fast enough to finish the entire area before any part of it dries. When it is finished it should be damp enough so that it shines, but not damp enough to have any pools. It will dry gradually, but until it is dry so that it does not come off on the finger, no other color can be put over it; therefore leave until later the windows or roof. Also, until it is dry, no other color area can be put adjacent to the first without their running together, unless a white line of dry paper is left between which is either to remain white or to be filled in later.

What is the next lightest item? It might be grass in sunlight—aureolin might be the proper color. It can be put in the same way as the house. Aureolin, also, might be the right color for the tree. In

painting in these two things, an interesting fact
may be noticed about the use of the flat brush. If
a hard uniform edge is wanted, such as a point
where the grass grows against the house, the tip
of the brush or the end away from you will give
it, as the brush moves sideways. The edge which
the heel of the brush makes, however, will be a
ragged edge caused by the flat of the hairs rubbing
across the grain in the paper. This difference can
be taken advantage of. When a ragged edge is
wanted, as might happen with the edge of the tree
or the grass growing against the sky or the foliage
of a tree, the pad can be turned around so that the
flat of the brush instead of the tip or side will define
the edge of the color. With the brush very dry and
held flatly and with fairly quick strokes instead of
measured ones, whole surfaces, as well as just the
edges, can be given this broken color effect. Fish-
nets or wet pavement are susceptible to the treatment as well as foliage. Note in Photograph II
the manner of holding the brush with a finger
pressed on the hairs to make them lie flat and touch
only the high spots on the paper. Leave plenty of
daylights or white spots; they will be used later
for filling in with a different quality of yellow or
green.

What is the next darker thing in the picture? It may be the sky. Suppose that it is shaded from light at the horizon to dark at the top and that Antwerp blue might, with different proportions of water, give the color and value. The sky is a larger area and will have to be put on wetter because it will take longer to cover it; and if we allow part of it to dry while the other part is wet, we shall have a bad hard edge where we do not want one; —that is between the dry and wet parts.

In wetting the brush, do not give it a shake as there should be plenty of water. Get a little blue on the brush and, turning the picture upside down, start outlining the house, chimney, etc., but do it quickly. Time is much more important than an accurate outline. Where the sky is adjacent to any darker area, let the color slop over as it will; the darker color will correct the edge later. As you quickly put on more brushfuls, add more and more color to the water. Tip the pad slightly toward you so that the outlined edges of the house are of even dampness, and there is a bead of water along the working edge which is approaching the lower edge of the pad. You are really drawing a pool of water tinctured with the color across the paper. In Photograph III, the blackish points are pools of water being constantly pulled down toward you as you work. The brush work for this whole area of sky, after you get the first irregularities of outline evened off, should be long horizontal sweeps, the full width of the brush and overlapping either side of the paper. You may have to pass the brush several times over the same path to avoid white specks.

In Photograph IV the brush has now gone back from the working edge to cover up some of these white specks. A few white specks are still visible at the left. Use swift horizontal strokes. Now with the dry-wiped brush, soak up any excessive bead of wetness along the bottom edge of the pad and keep the pad tilted toward you slightly all the time until dry. If you have worked quickly enough and used brushfuls of uniform wetness, you will get an even tint. If it is too light your brush carried too much water and not enough color; if it is too dark, more water and less color should have been used. Antwerp blue is a very strong color; a dried particle on the brush might account for a dark horizontal streak. If white pimples of bare paper show, your brush may have been too dry or held too flatly, or the strokes may have been too fast. If a balloon-like sharp edge shows halfway up the area, after drying, it is because your brush was too dry at the

III

In the first part of a tint or wash the brush is so wet that dark pools of water form on the near edge. The outline of the horizon and house is nearly completed.

IV

The last part
of the tint is
done with long
h o r i z o n t a l
strokes. Note
the dark pool
or rim of color
being drawn
across the pa-
per.

start, or you took too long, or were too painstaking with your outlines, and allowed the first part to dry so that it acted like a wick and absorbed back wet paint put on later.

Now is the moment for a wave of discouragement, because, unless the sky is evenly tinted and graded from light to dark, it is a failure. You might sponge out a cloud where there is a particularly murky spot, or you might like the unevenness or persuade yourself that a uniformly tinted sky is not a necessity, or you might go charlatan and put in some unrelated item to astonish the world. But, thinking of the picture as an exercise, unless the tint is even, you haven't done what you set out to do.

Handling a wash or tint, as it is sometimes called, is a basic part of watercolor painting. Unless one can do it, one will have trouble in controlling the smaller washes or making tints which grade properly from one color or value to another. This process should be learned at the outset so that whatever variations and irregularities occur will be due to intention rather than to mischance. There is enough of the involuntary in watercolors at best. Some accidents, in fact, are often the making of a picture, or the inception of a new style. One painter, a few years ago, noticed that drops of clear water falling on a partly dried area of color expressed the dappling on horses and deer and developed a kind of picture in which the discovery was exploited with great charm and effect.

In practising skies and big flat washes on the back of old pictures, try different colors. Ultramarine, turquoise, lemon yellow—you will find that they work out differently, and you will get used to them singly and in pairs. For instance, after getting a good tint with Antwerp blue, try one graded from light lemon yellow and a trace of Antwerp to darker Antwerp blue. Then try putting in a purple "mare's tail" cloud with *one stroke* of a fairly dry brush while the ground is still wet. All sorts of interesting results will develop as you work.

Do not be discouraged if even after many attempts you are unable to get an even wash. Most good watercolorists have spoiled hundreds of sheets of paper in the process.

The sign-painter's flat-stroke brush of ox-hair is the best for the purpose; and the rough paper, if not Fabriano's (which, by the way, is ideal for some other purposes) is better than the smooth; because the surface is full of little valleys which

V

With the brush held almost flat on the paper (at an angle of perhaps 10 or 15 degrees), the tip makes a smooth edge and the heel a ragged one.

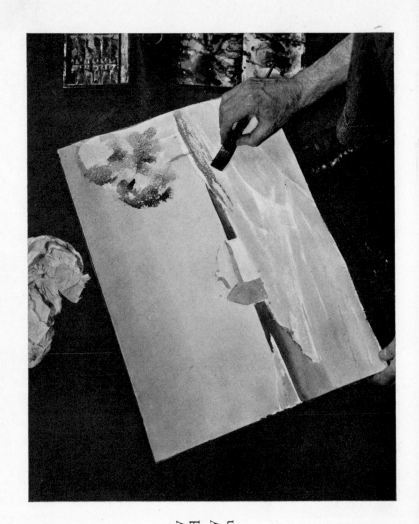

VI
A very dry
brush held
rather flatly
gives broken
color.

hold pools of color and retain the necessary moisture long enough to help you cover the entire surface before the first part is dry.

The next darker value in our picture is the shadow side of the house, the shadow of the chimney and shadow under the eaves, also the distant land. They can be done with the proper colors in the same way as the house in sunlight. (See Photograph I). Notice how the yellow-green grass casts its color up into the shadows under the eaves.

The ocean varies in value from the lighter color reflected from the sky in the bay near by to the darker horizon. In the example we are following through, the colors used were Antwerp blue with dark French blue run in at the horizon. Note the manner of holding the brush to get a sharp level line. The brush moves from left to right. The tip of the brush gave a sharp line (horizon), the heel or flat of the brush with the same stroke gave a ragged line (edge between the grass and distant ocean). This wash started in fairly wet in the foreground but had to be dryer toward the horizon in order to make the latter dark enough.

Always proceeding from the lighter to the darker values, we next come to the shadow side of the trees and the shadows of the trees and house on the grass. Choose the color which, put on over the yellow green, will best render the desired color. It will probably be one of the blues. For this operation the brush should be squeezed dryer than for any other so far. See in Photograph VI how flatly against the paper the brush is held. Have you noticed that the light spots on the ground made by sunlight coming through chinks in the leaves of a tree are often round or elliptical in shape? I have a wisteria vine screening a south porch which casts perfectly round silver dollars of light on the floor.

The color of shadows is varied by the nearest reflecting surface. Such a tree as ours would probably have bluer shadows where it is most exposed to the blue sky on top, but the underneath shadows would have some orange or yellow or brown resulting from reflection of the sun on any grass or road beneath the tree.

The trunks and branches of the trees, although very dark, could be put in next, because we might want them to run in slightly with the—still wet— shadow parts of the tree. You might like to shift to a smaller brush for this, but it is good practice to do it with the larger one. To make fine lines, hold the brush vertically to the paper as in Photo-

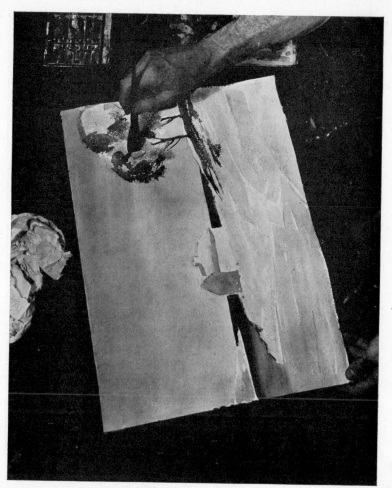

VII

Fine lines may be made with a large flat brush if it is held vertically and touched to, rather than stroked on, the paper.

VIII

With the corner of the brush scrubbed sideways one can obtain half-tone effects.

graph VII. If the fine line is to be curved, shape the brush into a curve with the left hand before touching it to the paper.

As the grass will probably not be of uniform color or value, parts of it can be gone over with slightly darker aureolin or some other yellow or green.

The half-tones in the rocks of the foreground are either bluish shadows reflected from the sky (if they face upwards) or reddish or orangey, if they face a sunlit area of lighted surface. These could be put in with a dry brush like the shadow parts of the tree. It will be a temptation to overdo them and cover too much of the first surface. *Resist the temptation and stop when there seem to be only half enough.*

Ripples or waves in the water on their far side reflect the lower sky, a color which comprises our first even wash. In the near side the waves reflect the higher sky of the zenith and also show some of the darker green from the underneath water into which we look. The nearer they are to us, the more we look down into their near side. Also the house and rocks will be reflected in the near or far side or both.

When you have determined the color to be used,

—the size of brush-stroke and the direction of the waves,—indicate them with quick and few strokes. They will look larger as well as darker as they come nearer. Although I used (in Photograph IX) the edge of the brush moving sideways, and had the waves coming towards me, there are no hard and fast rules for water or any other thing to be painted. Whatever shape or size the ripples or waves are, whatever direction they take, and whatever colors they may reflect from the sky or ocean bed; there is some kind of brush-stroke and pigment to match them. It is your job to discover the combination.

The darker accents in the rocks come next in value, also the shadow of the chimney and details like the dark places under the eaves. They will vary in color, and the size and shape of the brush-strokes will vary according to their respective characters. Since, however, they are darker than most things which have gone before, there should be less water in the brush and more color.

As the picture progresses, we may wish to modify some color already put on, such as, for instance, the yellow of the house. We can do it since as yet it contains no dark spots like windows. But to put a second wash of color over one already on always has a deadening effect.

IX

The tip of the brush quite wet and m o v e d s i d e w a y s makes a clean, sharp - edged stroke.

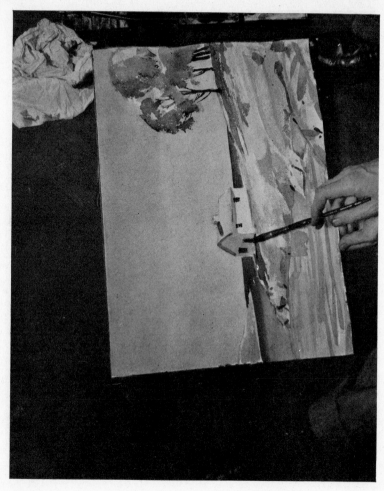

X

In this case a
half-inch brush
was used in-
stead of a one-
inch brush, al-
though for
windows this
size a larger
one would
have served
equally well.

Two weak coats of yellow or any other color will be much less crisp and brilliant than one stronger coat put on originally. Something seems to happen aside from the fuzzy and worked-over appearance which double edges give. If possible, get on plenty of color the first time. This will be difficult at first because all colors look darker when they are wet than after they are dry. *It is most important, therefore, to make everything, especially the darker values, a shade or two darker and more intense in color than you want them to look in the end.**

Darkest of all, and consequently the last thing to put in, are the windows and doors of the house. If the house has eight windows, three or four should be enough unless you are an architect or are doing a portrait of the house for the owner. If you can choose the windows that are characteristic and suggest the others, so much the better. The putting in of detail: rocks, trees, waves, etc., is like the use of words in English. Your picture can be redundant. It can contain much that is irrelevant; as in the style of Sinclair Lewis, it can say too much about a given thing. Leave out whole "paragraphs" of stuff

* Notice how the side of the house originally put on in Photograph I has lightened in successive pictures up to Photograph V,—a drying period of about 15 minutes.

that do not contribute to your characterization. The simpler and more powerful you make your statement, the stronger will be its appeal. Compare the several page accounts in any encyclopædia under the river Congo with the last four lines of Conrad's "Heart of Darkness":

"The offing was barred by a black bank of clouds, and the tranquil waterway leading to the uttermost ends of the earth flowed sombre under an overcast sky—seemed to lead into the heart of an immense darkness."

The first is informative, and probably interesting. I haven't read it. The passage from Conrad gives an emotion. It is pregnant with suggestion— as your painting should be.

Watercolors, however, should not be literary. A lone figure plodding his way home won't do any more. What you suggest should be not what some individual may be going to do or has done, but what the beholder would feel about the place if he were on that road.

CHAPTER II

MATERIALS AND THEIR USES

Papers

SINCE we have no white on our palette, we are dependent on the whiteness of the paper, clear, for absolutely white patches, or showing through the semi-transparent washes in the lighter areas. On this account we need the whitest possible paper.

It is a fact apparently not realized by salesmen in most of the art stores that the different batches of paper shipped them by the manufacturers vary in whiteness. Two lots of the same brand, grade, and surface will sometimes have quite a different degree of whiteness. This may be seen by laying a sample from an old lot on a fresh piece and holding them in a good light. Sometimes the old will be whiter or darker or they may be the same. Keep a sample of the whitest of each make to take with you when you buy paper. The discoloration is mostly towards ivory or yellow with the result that a clear bright blue or violet is difficult of attainment.

For the foregoing experiments I have recommended a heavy rough Whatman or Canson paper. Crisbrook, R.W.S., Arnolds, and many other papers are good. I mention these not because they are better but because I have tried them and am more familiar with them. Rough papers are easy to cover evenly with a tint, or large area of plain color, because the grain or rough surface is composed of very small ridges and valleys. As the wet brush passes over the ridges, an even amount of color comes off and the valleys retain dots of wetness. If not too much water is used it is prevented from flowing by gravity and by the fact that the thinner coats of color on the ridges dry more quickly. For a painting where erasures or corrections may have to be made, Canson is probably the best, as it has the hardest surface and is slower to soften and peel under an eraser, sponge, or cloth.

Another interesting paper is the heaviest and roughest D'Arches. It is really a cardboard and does not need to be in the form of a pad. Its surface is slightly darker and pinkish in color instead of yellowish like the other five. It is also the most absorbent. For this reason, it is suited to work just after sunset or on a cold or rainy day. Since the water is blotted or absorbed into the paper less time is lost in waiting for an area to dry. The staining colors blot into it very thoroughly, being almost impossible to weaken or get off, but the pigment or sediment colors remain on the surface and can be more easily removed.* This difference in the way the kinds of colors act on the D'Arches paper suggests interesting experiments, for a sky can be tinted with cerulean or French blue (pigment colors). After it is dry, clouds can be put on with water and a touch of alizarin crimson, madder, or alizarin orange, or some other staining color. While the cloud is still wet, blot up with a blotting paper and wipe carefully with a cloth and it will be found that most of the particles of blue have been removed where it was wet. But the paper underneath has absorbed sufficient of the water charged with the pink staining color to give an orange or pink area lighter in value and varying in color according to the amount of water, the delicacy of wiping, or the kind of staining color, used.

Fabriano is another most interesting paper widely used in America, as well as in European countries. As the surface of the rough-grained quality is much

* Note: See section on "Colors by Qualities," page 53.

rougher than any other, it is well adapted to dry brush work. Although, like most papers, it varies in whiteness, it is generally the whitest of all the papers, probably because it is made in Italy, where there is a lot of sun for natural bleaching, rather than in the north where there is almost none. For bright-colored sketches where a rough surface is desirable, Fabriano serves a useful purpose. Its chief disadvantage is that it is extremely soft as to surface and, once scraped or bruised, it takes color unevenly.

The smooth or hot-pressed papers are difficult to work. All the moisture from the brush is free to run to the lowest part of the wet brush-stroke and thus make a dark pool. A *thin* smooth paper should not be used even in a pad because the cockling or waving of the paper when it becomes wet makes much more trouble from pools than in the case of rougher papers.

Thin, smooth paper may be used in the studio where it can be glued on a drawing board, or for outdoors it can be bought ready-mounted on a cardboard.

Colors are much more brilliant on smooth paper than on rough. The rougher the paper the duller the colors become because each lump or ridge in the grain casts a shadow of its own, thus throwing a veil of grayness over the whole surface.

Hot-pressed, smooth paper also has the quality of not allowing the colors to adhere very closely. The pigment colors will wash off almost entirely, leaving white or slightly discolored paper; and even the staining colors loosen when a new wet brushstroke is superimposed over a color, although the last may be quite dry.

A German paper called "Drawingart," while not handmade, is claimed to be entirely of linen rags. It is cheaper than the others and a very interesting paper to use because though rough it has a hard surface. It is evidently given this roughness by a calender or some mechanical means instead of by a wire mesh. The interesting point for us is that the grains are rounding instead of steep-sided, allowing (with the hard surface) the wet color to run. It combines some of the advantages and disadvantages of both smooth and rough paper.

Colored or tinted papers are more interesting to the worker in gouache than to the watercolorist. If one puts Chinese white in watercolor it can become a solid covering color, known variously as gouache, tempera, or body color. Interesting effects may be achieved with it, but it is more nearly related to oil painting than to watercolor. It can be handled just as oil colors are with bristle brushes or a knife. Gouache is much simpler to use than watercolor because, as in oils, one can paint over or correct a mistake without much trouble. It is a frequent refuge for oil painters who wish to exhibit watercolors but have not the patience or time to learn true watercolor technique. If body color is used, it should either be used throughout, or confined to high lights or rare accents; otherwise one may be accused of avoiding a difficulty or of trying to cover a mistake. The covering up of mistakes, like fortunate accidental effects, is legitimate but should appear part of the intention rather than proclaim itself as a reconstruction. A woman's face with make-up only on one side and not the other would be noticeable and false, but if the touching up were evenly done, it might escape attention.

Tinted Papers

Tinted papers are made in 15 or 20 shades: cream, grays, ivory, etc. The difficulty for the watercolorist is that their colors are all standard and evenly tinted. One can make one's own tinted papers by soaking a white paper with a sponge and then squeezing the sponge dry and wiping off the excess moisture until the surface is evenly damp. Then paint on a light wash of staining color and immediately after wipe off a second time with the squeezed-out sponge. An even tint can be put over the entire paper in this way, and it will be a tint of your own choosing. It may be lighter on one side and darker on the other if wanted, or vary from one color to another. If the tinted foundation is to be used for a sky, then sweeping clouds can also be put in while it is still wet, if you wipe quickly enough and have not too much moisture or color in the brush.

The difficulty with this method is that, if there is much slightly darker color to go over this foundation after it is dry, the new wetness will loosen the foundation in some places more than others. This may be avoided by using, instead of watercolors, indelible colored inks which are not affected by water after they once dry. As many of the colored inks fade in the sunlight rather rapidly, they should be tested first. This loosening of a foundation tint can also be avoided by blowing a light coating of fixative on the paper after the tinting and before the next darker patches are applied.

There is, moreover, no reason for not putting a little color in the fixative if the entire surface of an otherwise finished picture needs a slightly different color. This corresponds to what is called glazing in oil painting and amounts in either medium to putting a veil of some modifying color over either the entire picture or a part of it. The oil painter can do it with a brush or cloth because the colors dry so hard that the new solvent does not dissolve them. This may be done with a fixative blower, or I have heard of using an atomizer with very diluted colored inks. In either case, practise the process first before trying it on a good picture. You will find it very easy to overdo this. As in suggesting windows or branches of trees, there is a temptation to be generous. Good taste requires the just too little or just too few.

Old pictures which you would otherwise throw away and of which you should accumulate at least a hundred in a summer's work are fine material for experiments of this kind.

Brushes

Brush work is more important in watercolor than in any other kind of painting. Find a brush that suits you and learn all the possible strokes it can make. Get large brushes rather than small ones—they can come to just as sharp a point or edge, and you can do just as fine and delicate detail work with them, and at the same time can quickly fill in a large area without losing precious time. Precious, because your first impression is usually valuable and is lost by changing lights or too prolonged looking at the subject you are working from. Precious, also, because when a color is put over another lighter one, it softens it, and repeated little strokes wear off the first color in some places and not others. Work quickly, if for no other reason than because speed will make you decisive and sure. You will make bad blunders and plenty of ugly strokes, but they are better than indecisive ones. More than with any other kind of art, a watercolor must seem to have been easily rather than laboriously done. Its spontaneity and dash are more important than other possible good qualities, and these come chiefly from working quickly.

When the brush is quite wet it will tint evenly on large areas. (See Photographs III and VI.) Tip the paper toward you slightly so that the pool or rim of water will hang on the near working edge, carry it right off the edge of the pad—if possible. If not, bring it to a corner of the tinted area and absorb it back into the brush by wiping the brush dry with the fingers. The brush when tinting these large areas should contain the amount of mixed water and color that it will normally hold.

For smaller areas, especially dark ones, there should be less water, about the amount of wetness that will result from dipping the brush in the water, touching it to a color in the box and then giving it a shake after the manner of a nurse with a thermometer. (See Photographs IX and X.) This is the normal brush-stroke. There is another degree of dryness which is equally important. For this dip the brush in the water, squeeze most of the water out by passing it lightly between the thumb and forefinger of the other hand, then get the color on it from a pigment in the box which has previously been moistened. This dry brush will touch the humps on a rough paper and leave a pattern of irregular untouched paper in the valleys. It is useful because it gives broken color and thus implies detail in bark, foliage, grass, stone, cloth, or in material with light glancing across it. For dry brush work, it is better to hold the brush as flat as possible on the paper—even place the forefinger on the hairs. (See Photographs II and VI.)

Practise on the back of old pictures brush-strokes with varying amounts of wetness in the brush and with the brush held at different angles. Try the corner of the brush, the edge, sideways; trail it, push it, pat with the side of it, press hard on it so that the heel of the brush scrubs the paper. Study the effects of these different strokes; try them with the brush as dry as a shake will make it or dryer by squeezing out additional moisture with the fingers. See if you can find in the patterns thus produced symbols for foliage, masonry, clouds or ripples in water. Try to utilize the symbol by employing it consciously on some detail. Study watercolors by other people and ask yourself how a certain stroke or effect could be produced. Study Chinese and Japanese painters when you have a chance—they are the greatest masters of brush work. Get any books available on Japanese brush work or water-color methods.

Sponge (as a tool)

Think of a sponge as a tool for getting original effects, not as a corrective for dark spots in tints or for working out mistakes. It is commonly used as a corrective, but the results are uncommonly bad.

If a sponge is to be used at all, it should figure as number one on the batting order. For foundation washes, skies, etc., the method is to wet the paper thoroughly, then squeeze the sponge dry, quickly absorbing all the water that it will naturally take up until the paper is uniformly damp but without pools. Apply the color with a large brush or the sponge itself as described under "tinted papers"; and then with parallel strokes or circular strokes repass the entire surface, working from the lightest to the darkest. If the foundation tint is a late sky graded from rose at the horizon through lemon yellow to blue, it may be necessary slightly to revolve the sponge in the hand en route in order not to mix the colors. All this must be done before any part becomes dry. Now while it is still wet is the time to put in a darker cloud with a fairly dry brush or to wipe out a lighter cloud with the sponge or brush cleaned and squeezed as dry as possible, or with a clean dry cloth.

Rubber Cement

In sponging or brushing in a sky, it is sometimes not possible to pay attention to the outlines or edges because the time taken to paint around an intricate edge would be so long that the first stroke would dry before the area was completed. Let us trace the stages in painting a picture where some lighter object is silhouetted against such a sky, like the trunk of a white birch tree or a cloud with hard outlines.

XI

Pencil indications of a picture in which white birch trees will be seen against a darker background. In the upper right hand corner rubber cement is being squeezed directly out of the tube on to the parts to be "stopped out."

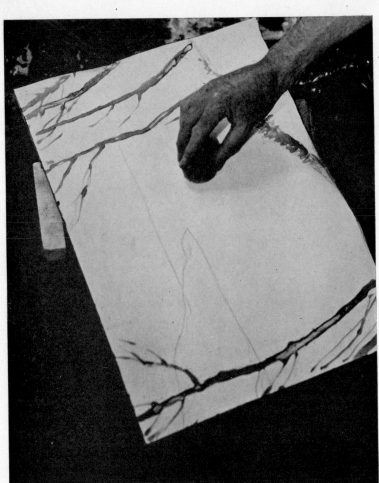

XII

While the rubber cement protects the paper under it, a light wash is being put on with a sponge. The wash is darkened before it is dry with brushfuls of whatever color is to surround the white trunks.

This can be accomplished by first covering the birch tree trunk with rubber cement. Ordinary tire patching cement in a tube will do—get it at any garage—or there is an illustrator's rubber cement at the art stores. It is difficult to use with a brush except on smooth paper. For rough paper it is better to squeeze it from the tube directly onto the paper. It should be put on in a fairly heavy coat or ridge for a thin tree trunk. As it dries it will flatten out and form a protective coating over the paper. You will find it difficult to handle and it has to be coaxed to make a sharp corner or a thin line. Be sure to use enough.

It will dry in about ten minutes. Then with a sponge or full brush, tint on your background, with the same long, firm, horizontal strokes that you would use if there were no cement. Ride right over it; even put a dark cloud behind the birch tree or, after the tint is dry, a distant hill or clump of trees. In Photograph XII the rubber cement looks lighter in value merely because it is dry. Any amount of work may be done over the rubber cement without disturbing it. In Photograph XIII, for instance, reflections and ripples in the water are crossing the birch trees which will later become pure white paper.

In Photograph XIV the cement is being removed with a piece of art gum. In this case we start with part of the foreground. Note the particles which come off the two birch trees. Staining colors are better to use as far as this point because they are less easily removed in peeling off or erasing the rubber cement.

Photograph XV shows the cement entirely removed, and from this point the completion of the picture is a matter of straightforward painting. The white paper in the trees and foreground can be colored. The branches and leaves, or the bands where bark has been peeled off, are things which I had started to do; but this particular picture done under the stress of comments and interruptions by the photographer, in making his exposures, hardly seemed worth finishing. While of no art value, the illustrations will serve to show you the possibilities of this method.

As a result of using rubber cement, all the parts, however intricate, even single leaves of a tree, if you go in for leaves, will be the original white paper. To have painted such an even sky or background around and in between would have been impossible.

Instead of rubber cement I have used, in covering

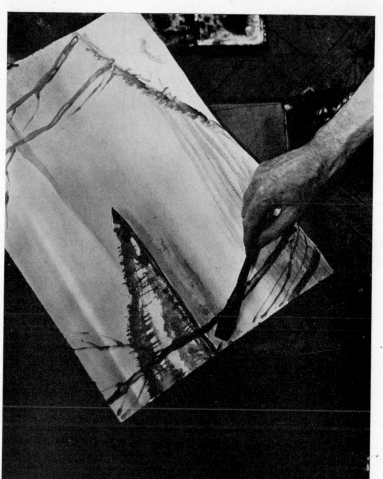

XIII

Even very dark colors may be painted over the rubber cement without danger of discoloring the insulated paper. Without the cement it would have been impossible to paint evenly around the trunks and branches.

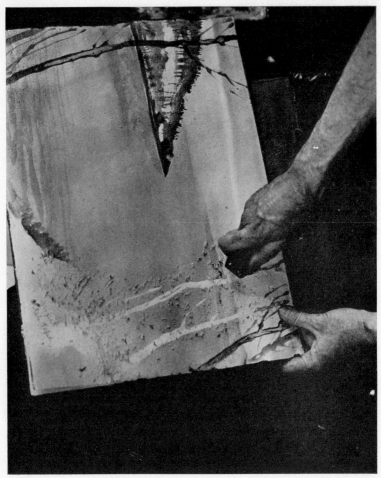

XIV

Art gum removes the rubber cement, leaving clear white paper. Note the particles of cement rubbed off the two trees and part of the foreground.

large areas, a material known as "Scotch tape." It is a thing made up for commercial photographers to hold plates for printing. It may be obtained at the larger photographic supply stores. Scotch tape is a paper ribbon with rubber cement on one side. It sticks very well to all but the roughest papers; waterproofs the area to be protected from coloring, and usually comes away clean. If traces of the cement adhere, they may be removed with art gum or kneaded rubber. A pair of scissors is useful in cutting the Scotch tape to the size and shape wanted.

Colors by Qualities

Paint is composed of three materials with three different functions: a powder or dye to give the color, a gum or glue to stick it to the paper, and a thinner (water) for varying the consistency for different kinds of brush-strokes.

The mineral, animal and vegetable kingdoms have been combed rather thoroughly to provide us with pigments, and both chemistry and the coal tar industries have recently contributed some valuable new ones. The paints made by any of the reliable manufacturers are all good in quality. Some painters prefer one make and some another; the preference no doubt being based as much on prejudice, imagination or habit, as on difference in quality.

Some of the colors fade in the light and should not be used,—usually the manufacturer classifies them as "not permanent." Sap green, cypress green, gamboge, carmine, yellow lake, mauve and most of the coal tar blues, violets and purples are such colors. Any manufacturer's catalogue will give you a complete list.

Other colors, while permanent by themselves, are bad in combination. Emerald green and chrome yellow are such colors. Still others are bad when used with only certain enemy colors. For this reason, it is better to do only what mixing is absolutely essential. Use the colors pure as much as possible, especially the brighter and lighter ones. Of necessity there will be some mixing and superimposing of colors. It is better to do this directly on the paper. Put a brushful of the dominant color and then modify it with a part brushful of whatever other color is necessary. Since all colors seem darker when first put on wet than after they are dry, allowance should be made by coloring everything apparently a little too dark.

All the colors may be divided into two classes:

XV

All the rubber cement is now removed and the picture is ready to be finished.

*what I call the pigment colors, and the staining
colors.* Pigment colors are the ones which contain
as coloring matter a powder or sediment of varying
degrees of fineness. These colors tint the paper by
depositing on it a layer of particles. They are difficult to tint with, easy to modify and remove with a
clean brush, and can be more easily erased with an
eraser after drying. The ones which have the coarsest
particles and hence are most noticeable for these
qualities are: cerulean blue, cobalt violet, emerald
green, cobalt blue, ultramarine, vermilion, ochres
and umber.

The staining colors are the ones which depend
on a dye, a stain, or an extremely fine dust—which
acts as a stain—for their covering quality. These
colors stain the surface of the paper rather than
deposit a layer of particles. The coal tar, alizarin
and madder colors are all of this nature, as are also
Prussian and Antwerp blue. These staining colors
are easy to tint with, but difficult to remove by wetting or with art gum or an eraser after they are
once dry.

The other colors range between these groups, but
all of them have more or less special qualities and
act in slightly different ways in mixtures with each
other. The student will have to try the different

ones and see which lend themselves better to whatever convention or style of work he is developing.

Possible Palettes

The choice of a palette depends on the kind of work to be done. For general outdoor painting it should include colors which will as nearly as possible render, either singly or by mixtures, all the hues of the spectrum and all the values in each hue from white to the darkest. It should also provide the opportunity of using each color in any degree of brilliancy from its point of greatest saturation to neutral gray. It should do these things with as little mixing as possible and should contain colors which are inactive with each other and which are unaffected by sunlight. This is a large order. The following three palettes are suggested as starting points in building a set of colors which will best serve your purpose. If you squeeze them out in the box in the order named from left to right, you will have the cold colors mostly on one side and the warm ones on the other. The dull colors listed in each case should go under the corresponding brilliant colors with black in the center under bright green.

PALETTE NO. I

All these colors are mutually inactive; that is, any one may be mixed freely with any of the others without fear of discoloration from chemical reactions. They are also chosen, at some sacrifice of brilliancy, for best permanence to light.

Bright Colors, Top Row

Cadmium Red
Brilliant Orange No. I (Schmincke)
Cadmium Yellow Medium
Aureolin
Lemon Yellow
Viridian
Cerulean Blue
Cobalt Blue
French Blue (Weber's)
Mineral Violet
Indian Red

Dull Colors, Bottom Row

Burnt Sienna	Ivory Black
Burnt Umber	Mars Violet
Roman Ochre	Davy's Gray

PALETTE NO. 2

In this palette brilliancy is the objective. It is accomplished at a small sacrifice of permanency to light, and certain of the colors should not be mixed—especially emerald green, which turns dark with French blue or orange vermilion.

Bright Colors, Top Row

Orange Vermilion
Cadmium Orange
Brilliant Yellow No. II (Schmincke) or Bright
  Yellow No. 3 (Talens)
Brilliant Yellow No. I (Schmincke) or Bright
  Yellow No. 2 (Talens)
Strontian Yellow or Lemon Yellow
Brilliant Yellow Green No. I (Schmincke or
  Talens)
Emerald Green
Brilliant Turquoise No. II (Schmincke) or Sea-
  green No. 2 (Talens)
Prussian Blue
French Blue (Weber's)
Brilliant Violet No. I (Schmincke)
Alizarin Crimson

Dull Colors, Bottom Row

Burnt Sienna   Payne's Gray
Sepia   Neutral Tint
Mars Yellow   Davy's Gray
Lamp Black

PALETTE NO. 3

This palette is cheaper than the other two, since the substitutions provide colors which are not as permanent or safe but are lower in cost.

Bright Colors, Top Row

Brilliant Orange No. II
Brilliant Orange No. I
Chrome Orange
Chrome Yellow Medium
Brilliant Yellow No. I
Brilliant Yellow Green No. II
Hooker's Green (Dark)
Brilliant Turquoise No. II
Prussian Blue
New Blue
Purple Lake
Alizarin Crimson

Dull Colors, Bottom Row

Indian Red   Ivory Black
Burnt Sienna   Indigo
Burnt Umber   Charcoal Gray
Yellow Ochre

Instead of this palette one could use Palettes No. 1 or 2, substituting tempera colors in tubes for the more expensive watercolors. Tempera tube colors are so nearly like watercolors that it is difficult to tell the difference without reading the label. They are not quite as brilliant and some of them are not quite as transparent. Use them from tubes as you would watercolors.

Most teachers of oil painting agree that a student should start with a very simple palette. The reason for this is to accustom him to mixing two colors to make a third and partly to prevent him (by limiting his range of brilliancy) from painting pictures that are not harmonious in color. Many professional painters themselves use a very simple palette. I have heard them cry in triumph: "There, I did it all with three colors." A limited palette, however, does not guarantee a simple and effective color harmony.

There are so many possibilities locked up in the wonderful range of pigments at our disposal that it is a pity to try only a few. The lists which I have given are merely a suitable starting point. Do not think of these palettes as permanent; as you go on working, replace whatever colors you find you are not using with new "undiscovered" ones. Let good taste in results be your guide rather than limitation of the pigments at your disposal. You may make unpleasing combinations, but if you recognize them as unpleasing, all is well. If you do not, you will, at any rate, be amusing yourself. We all produce painful effects from time to time. What a heartening thing it would be to students if they could see the failures of our best painters! I am afraid self-abasement is not prevalent enough to lead us ever to expect to see an exhibition to which each would send his most atrocious color scheme. Look at your worst sketch before you destroy it or experiment with it. And rest assured that many professional watercolorists, some of them famous, have done things just as bad.

Colors by Makes or Brands

Test colors against fading in the light by artificially ageing them in the sun. To do this, put an even wash an inch or so wide on a piece of paper beside other such washes, label them with the name of the color and cover up half by clipping on a heavy dark paper or metal or wooden cover, then place the sample sheet in a southern window where it will get direct sun for several weeks. On uncovering the other half, one can see what effect the sun has had.

Among the Weber, Newman, Bourgeois, Le Franc, Winsor Newton, Devoe, Romney and Horadam colors which I have tested in the sun, I have found the following colors which either faded or changed: Italian pink, marine blue, saffron, mauve, violet lake, magenta, transparent green blue, purple madder, transparent blue, cypress green, sap green, geranium, Indian yellow, rose catharme, carmine. Among the all coal tar colors tested,—Schmincke "Light-proof," Pelikan "Eilida," Talens "Bright Series," so-called Japanese inks, and several other kinds of colored inks,—the ones which have faded in the light are all the cool colors in the spectrum from red to yellowish green, especially the blues and violets. The warm colors, particularly the yellows and oranges, are apparently light-proof. Although they fade slightly in strong sunlight, I frequently use Schmincke's turquoise no. II or Talens seagreen because they are splendid bright colors. It is unusual to hang paintings in the direct sunlight. When I use them, moreover, I mix in a little Antwerp blue—the result is a color which has some of the brilliancy of the coal tar color and some of the stability of the Antwerp blue.* No painter can get brilliant effects without occasionally using a fugitive color, sometimes without being aware that he is using it.

The following colors fade or change color slightly; but they are permanent enough so that most watercolorists use them freely. They are colors which are almost essential and for which, either on account of brilliancy or other special qualities there are no better substitutes: alizarin crimson, Antwerp blue, cadmium orange, neutral tint, Payne's gray, Prussian blue, rose madder, sepia, vermilion and orange vermilion.

My preference in makes of colors is probably prejudice or habit. I like the Weber or the English cadmiums (Winsor Newton or Newman), the Weber French blue, and the Schmincke "Lightproof" for aniline or coal tar colors, that is those of them which are sun-proof, the yellows and oranges and yellow greens. Among the aniline colors— either oil or aquarelle—I have never seen any absolutely sun-proof turquoise blues or purples or violets. With such rapid strides, however, as have lately

* This mixture is now put up by Schmincke under the name of "O'Hara Blue."

been made by the manufacturers, these few exceptions may soon join the large group of unalterable colors.

CHAPTER III

CORRECTIONS

ALTHOUGH there should not be any corrections in a successful watercolor, its success
may sometimes actually depend on some minor
alteration. Just as it is very good training, as a matter of discipline, to attend a drawing class without
an eraser, or to write a page of prose without ad-
jectives, it is good training in watercolor work to
place one's self in the position of thinking of mistakes as irretrievable. Most of them actually are; but
there are a few corrections which can be practised,
preferably after the painting is otherwise finished.
Do not stop to fiddle with minor inaccuracies while
the impulse is fresh. A good watercolor should not
take more than an hour of fast concentrated work;
while the conditions which drew you to that particular subject still stimulate you. Afterwards, at
home, as you look at the picture and seek to evalu-
ate it and wonder what might have been done
better, you will possibly see occasion for some of the

following procedures. The chances are fifty-fifty against spoiling the picture, but I give them in the interest of completeness.

Dark touches can, of course, be put in over the light areas. It is the light corrections over dark which give trouble and are dealt with here.

Erasures of Different Kinds

Construction marks in pencil put on before the colors, may be removed with a piece of art gum without greatly disturbing the colors. This is especially true of the staining colors—the sediment colors sometimes are inclined to loosen. In the dark parts of the picture such pencil lines do not show, but sometimes in a high light their removal freshens the effect.

Careful erasing with an ordinary soft eraser will lighten colors, but this is difficult to do evenly in large areas.

An ink eraser or gum with an abrasive in it will remove most of the color from the high spots in the paper and leave it in the valleys. This, of course, gives a speckled effect.

Sandpaper will act like an ink eraser, but more violently.

Such effects as those of the sun drawing up water

The sun draws up water by means of a straight-edge
and an eraser.

XVII

This shows the
alternate use
of a brush with
plenty of clear
water in it and
a dry cloth.
The longer the
interval be-
tween wetting
and wiping the
more of the
ground color
will be re-
moved.

or casting rays, of dust particles in the air, or of light streaming through the window of a church interior, may be achieved with a straight-edge and an eraser—the straight-edge by protecting what it covers gives a sharper line than could be obtained with an eraser alone. A stencil for a curve or corner can be cut out of thin metal to give a sharp line when erasing.

All tinkering with erasures gives a mottled area on rough paper not wholly in keeping with the rest of the picture.

Bristle Brush

Any color may be lightened by carefully scrubbing with water and a bristle brush such as oil painters use. Use fresh water and stand by with a cloth to blot up from time to time the paint which has been loosened. Although this method leaves an even surface, there is usually a dark line around the edge of the area treated.

Brush, Cloth and Art Gum

Any color can be entirely removed from all hot-pressed and most rough paper, but not from rough Fabriano or D'Arches (which have too soft surfaces) by the following method: With pure water in your watercolor brush, paint over the area to be made white again. Use plenty of water on the area to be removed, but do not wet or dampen the adjacent parts of the painting. Have the water fairly evenly distributed over the area. Leave it wet for a few minutes. You will find a tendency for it to dry first in the corners or thin lines. Wet it again there if necessary. With cloth or blotting paper drink up the water until the area is merely damp. With a dry part of the cloth, briskly rub across the entire area and adjacent parts, and quickly before it dries more rub with the art gum. The recently wet place will come off clean without disturbing the surrounding thoroughly dry parts. Pure white paper will result unless parts of the wet place have dried too much. The white spot or line is always a trifle wider than the part actually wet with the brush for removal; that is because it is inclined to spread a little, owing to a small amount of water being absorbed out into the apparently dry rim. This tendency may easily be allowed for after a little practice.

A variation of this is a method of making clouds or white steam coming from a chimney. Paint the entire cloud and wipe off without letting the water stay on too long. You will notice that the background has been lightened perceptibly. The longer you let the water remain the more comes off. By light rubbing at the top and harder rubbing near the chimney, with perhaps a touch of a soft eraser at points, a nicely graded bleaching can be accomplished in the case of white smoke or steam. (See Photograph XVII.)

Sponge (as a corrective)

A sponge will remove the darkest color, but will leave a ragged edge unless it is handled carefully. When a part has been sponged it will not be pure white paper but gray in color, and unless the place can be crisply painted over, the effect will be bad. Use this only as a last resort. While sponging, it is well to have a clean dry cloth in the left hand to wipe dry as the color becomes sufficiently loosened. This prevents a bad edge. I spoil nineteen out of twenty pictures which I try to sponge into shape.

Fixative Blower

Oil painters do what is called glazing, by which is meant putting a transparent veil or thin layer of color over the entire surface or part of the surface of an otherwise finished picture. The effect is to darken all the values and to make the whole more yellow, rosy or blue according to the color used. It is extremely difficult to blow colored fixative on a paper evenly and this should be practised first on old pictures or paper. The tendency will be to put in too much color at first and to get too much water on the paper.

Chalk and Colored Pencils, Charcoal, Pen and Ink

Some watercolorists use chalk, pastel or colored pencils to cover up mistakes in a watercolor or to get effects not otherwise obtainable. This can be easily done, but the picture should be fixed afterwards with fixative like a pastel. My objection to this practice is on the same grounds as my objection to the use of body color, that the work becomes no longer a watercolor but a work in mixed mediums, partly a pastel and partly a watercolor. It is probably ethical—anything is ethical in the mechanism of art—if the result justifies the means. In other words, do it if you can get away with it.

Wax Pencils

Colored wax pencils such as are given to children to play with will, if put on the paper before the paint is applied, make lines upon which the watercolor will not "take." Thus a screen or grill can be put over the entire surface of the paper or parts of it. Fine twigs of trees, lines of rain, animal or bird cages, texture of cloth, etc., may be indicated with wax pencils of the proper color.

Chinese White

Chinese white is the one body color which so many watercolorists have employed that its use has become an accepted practice. It is suitable for high lights, reflections, etc., and does not detract from the watercolor, if it is not over-used or mixed with other colors to make the watercolor resemble an oil or a gouache.

Penknife

A better way of putting in highlights or trimming up a bad, dark edge against light is with a razor blade or sharp knife. A "v"-shaped cut or surface scratch will pick out white lights very effectively.

Burnisher

In using rough paper it is sometimes convenient to make a small section of the paper smooth. This may be done with an agate burnisher or a rounded steel like the handle of a pair of scissors.

A picture of mine in the Watercolor Collection of

the Brooklyn Museum called "Noonday Glare" is an example of this. To render the glitter of the sun on the water near the horizon the purest white was desired. Burnishing did away with the lumps on the paper and consequently with the shadow cast by each lump. (See photograph opposite.)

On occasions when a color looks opaque and shouldn't, a burnisher is also useful. Light rubbing will render it more transparent.

XVIII

"NOONDAY
GLARE"

This illustrates
two points: the
use of a bur-
nisher for
whites, and of
a mat shaded
from dark to
light to over-
emphasize the
sun's glare on
the left.

CHAPTER IV

STUDIO WORK ON OUTDOOR SUBJECTS

COLLECTORS and connoisseurs of watercolors sometimes ask if they were done on the spot, the notion being that if they had been done there rather than at the studio there would be more snap and character to them. This is sometimes true, but not always. Many painters of landscape do more "outdoorsy" work at home from sketches taken in the field than they do on the spot. Perhaps it is because the sketch reminds them of the important characteristics of a place, time of day or feeling, and they forget the unimportant ones. This elimination of the unimportant may be a sifting in the memory, and may with certain people be better than the conscious attempt (on the spot) to record only that which contributes to the character of the subject.

Of course, if one worked only in the studio, one would lose contact with new sources of inspiration and work more and more to formula. Indeed, many who do work entirely inside after their first years of gathering material and experience betray it in their product. In any event, "working up" pictures at home is at least worth trying. In the first place, there is no need of tampering with the original sketch. Start a new one from it. After several pencil plans of different variations you find that you can or cannot improve the composition. In either case the procedure is the same as with the outdoor sketch. It should be done in the same short time—possibly one hour—and with the same freedom. You will have plenty of clean water and a table (waist high) to work on instead of squatting in the sun. You will have a much wider range of pigments. A dull red that was had before by mixing orange vermilion with black or some other color, may now be chosen as light red, Venetian red, or Mars red, and will ring true. A shadow that you made too dark and uniform can be enlivened by a reflected light, if theory or taste make an excuse for it, or indeed without any excuse if it improves the color pattern.

The paper should be horizontal as when it is on the ground outdoors and the light should come from as high as possible, preferably from overhead.

A Larger Palette

For the studio a large palette with a wide choice

of colors gives flexibility and quick selection. The palette can be set up like the outdoor box according to the spectrum, split at the red to bring the cold colors on one side and the warm ones on the other; but there will be more colors, more space. They may be arranged in three or four rows, along the top the brightest ones and also those which by their nature should not be mixed (orange vermilion, chrome yellow, and emerald green.)

In the second row place colors which can be mixed if necessary, some of them as bright as the top row, others not quite as bright (the warm coal tar colors,—reds and yellows, Antwerp blue, ultramarine, mineral violet).

In the third, duller or grayer pigments corresponding in the spectrum to the ones over them. (Siennas, umbers, dull reds, ochres, the Mars colors, dull greens, Payne's gray, neutral tint, black sepia.)

With as complete a palette as this there is rarely any mixing; you can almost put your brush right on the desired spot as regards intensity or shade. Ladyfinger pans or candy pans at the Five and Ten Cent Stores, enameled white with Duco, make good large-sized palettes, two squeezes to each ladyfinger.

Photographs

I sometimes take a photograph after completing an outdoor sketch which looks as if it had possibilities for later development. I say this realizing that it will evoke the scorn of many painters who suppose that the intention is to copy the photograph. The snap is often quite valuable as raw material. You can eliminate from a photograph as well as from nature and it often supplies a detail or surface appearance which is invaluable. With such a sketch, I sometimes make a pencil drawing or two, varying the composition slightly in each. These drawings often give me a better composition than the color sketch. The photograph and pencil drawing, as well as the sketch, serve to freshen the memory and reawaken the first impression.

A Pocket Recorder

How often you see something you would like to paint when you haven't your materials with you! Look as you will, it is difficult to impress it upon the mind sufficiently to go home and record it. For this reason, I make a practice of carrying a small watercolor set in the side-pocket of my car. It is small enough to go in an overcoat pocket as well. There are a 4 x 6 inch pad, a ¼ inch flat brush, and a child's paint box with seven or eight brilliant colors and black. With color notes (small rough pictures) this size and a pencil drawing on another sheet, a fleeting moment may be saved for posterity or the family waste basket.

Spotting a Figure

Many watercolorists have the knack of placing a dark accent—a window, boat or figure—in exactly the right spot. This often evokes the comment: "He does it by instinct, something subconscious, casual, but unerring." Those who have overheard such flattering remarks and know them to be undeserved may smile. Here is my best method for putting a figure on the spot. First make the figure or several figures in slightly different sizes on another piece of paper. Cut them out roughly with scissors and tack up the picture across the room, then "pin the tail on the donkey" in various places and with various-sized figures or groups of figures until they cannot be more satisfying as to size or position. Leave them over night if you are not sure, then either mark around them or paint them in from head and foot marks.

CHAPTER V

GENERAL NOTES

1. Lightening a Color

SOMETIMES when a sky or sea is being painted one will notice an uneven appearance or dark spot, or the whole may be too dark in value. All of it or parts can be lightened, if, *before it is quite dry,* a soft cloth is passed very lightly over the surface, almost trailed across. Move it toward the edge of the paper and away from any outlining of horizon, trees, or roofs.

2. Pauses

Stand back, while you are working, and look at the picture from time to time during the drying periods. This will help form an idea of the next move. Three intermissions in the course of a painting are quite likely to prevent three false moves.

3. Delayed Drying

If you wish to spend more time on a part of the picture than is allowed by the natural drying time, a little library paste or watercolor medium (called megilp) may be added. Some prefer glycerine. Many painters use a lot of paste but the effect while interesting is somewhat different from that of a normal watercolor. All these things are worth trying; you may find in some such procedure exactly the technique which suits you best.

4. Painting in the Cold

When painting at an altitude or in cold weather, a waterproof glove on the left hand is a comfort as this hand is constantly used for squeezing extra water and color out of the wet brush. On days below freezing, the color sometimes freezes on the paper. This may be avoided by adding a little salt or alcohol to the water. Salt is better as the alcohol interferes with normal brush work.

5. Brush Drill

A wet brush puts on a lot of water, containing either a smaller or larger amount of color. A dryer brush puts on less water, but the percentage of color in the water may be so great as to leave a darker stroke on the paper than would a wet brush. If the brush is clean and squeezed dry, it will blot up or absorb water from the wet paper; with the absorbed water it will take up an equal proportion of the color which was mixed with the water. It is therefore possible while the paper is still wet to add to or take away colors from a given area or to flood in an additional color, allowing them to run together. The wetter the area, the more the new color will blend or run in. A small amount of well-directed practice in modifying a wet area of color will greatly strengthen your brush work.

For instance, put on a medium wet stroke of blue, then with the dry clean brush absorb part of the color from one end. Do this again and instead of bleaching one end, strengthen it by a dry brush charged with stronger blue. Next try a third bleaching and, immediately adding some orange or red, bleach the latter color. Devise studies of this kind and watch the results for useful tricks applicable to landscape.

6. Framing

In framing a watercolor some have a preference for a close frame and others for a mat, either white or some plain color. The frame and mat are as much a part of the picture as any of the color areas or "spots" put in with the brush. The painter alone should be the judge of how his picture is to be presented. Experiments should be made with different colors of moulding and different mat materials. The width of the mat or its color will often either make or break the whole impression. While it is usual to make the mat all of one value and hue, it is interesting to try shading the mat differently on one side and the other or from top to bottom. For example, imagine a painting wherein bright sunlight is implied glittering on water at the left side of the picture, the right side being darker. If the mat were tinted darker on the left side the effect would be to heighten the glitter of the water. What takes place in this case is an optical illusion. The mind assumes that the mat is all of one value, because mats usually are; therefore the eye sees the sunlit water as lighter than it is really painted. If the mat is subtly shaded you can thus increase your possible range of values beyond black and white and achieve a color apparently more saturated in any given value than the one you have actually used. (See Photograph XVIII.)

The same process will work with hues as well as values: a blue sky may be seemingly intensified without using a more brilliant kind of blue, by tinting the top part of the mat which is juxtaposed with the sky very slightly with orange (the complementary color of blue) and the other half very slightly gray or even blue.

7. Care of Pictures

Watercolors should naturally be covered with a clear quality of glass and the crack between the glass and the wood of the frame should be sealed all around with a thin piece of gummed paper or cloth tape. This keeps out moisture in a damp climate and coal gas in an overheated or poorly ventilated room. Framers in the United States usually neglect this precaution although they frequently seal up the crack between the wooden frame and the usual wooden or cardboard backing.

CHAPTER VI

REMARKS ON UTILIZING TECHNIQUE

WHILE I have thus far purposely refrained from any generalizations on painting, the following remarks may be helpful. Some of these are original but many of them are quoted from conversations with other painters, or books on art, which, by the way, are nearly all interesting and should be read by the student in order that he may have at his disposal a choice of the accumulated prior thought. I would give credit to the ones quoted, but memory is not infallible and I fear I should misstate the remarks of some painter or author.

Don'ts

Don't choose a complicated subject with too many things in it. Simpler ones are better and easier.

Don't use small brushes.

Don't mix more than two colors together in the box. Mix them on the paper by applying successive alternate brushfuls.

Don't, more than is absolutely necessary, super-impose one color on another already dry. They lose brilliancy.

Don't look too frequently at the subject because you will become obsessed with unimportant things.

Don't spend more than an hour on one water-color.

Don't forget to clean your brush between colors.

Don't walk past a subject that appeals to you looking for a better one. You may walk miles without finding it and get into a frame of mind when nothing seems good enough.

Don't be discouraged.

The object of painting is so to dispose areas of color within a frame that they will give the beholder the strongest possible emotion. There are various conventions which different groups of painters observe. These groups are all interested in various kinds of formal composition (arrangement). We have the conventions of the Japanese print-maker; the standard rules of the older European painters which have been copiously discussed in art books; the countless "isms" of the last few decades: dynamic symmetry of line, space and color; plastic recession and cubic conception. Some of these theories will live and others not, but they are all most interesting to the art student and should be studied and used when appropriate.

In arranging your composition the size, shape and color of a spot of paint may be more important than what the spot represents. You may, nevertheless, have occasion to wish a spot to be recognized as some particular thing. This can often be done merely by carefully drawing in some characteristic detail of the thing or by inventing an easily recognizable symbol for it.

With trees, for instance, there are certain characteristic lines and treatments which, in most people's minds, denote a certain kind of tree. It may be useful to you if I roughly sketch the set which I have found helpful, in order that you need not worry the observer by making him try to account, for instance, for a palm tree beside a New England barn, where he might have been prepared to see an apple or an elm. Such an anomaly, of course, would not trouble those who think in terms of sheer design or color: for them it need not be a tree at all.

Symbols and Brush-strokes for Twelve Kinds of Trees

The following illustrations show, in each case, a possible symbol to have in mind while painting the tree.

In the middle row are practice strokes or related brush-drill.

In the bottom row the strokes and symbols are utilized in producing sample trees.

Like many things in this book, these are not entirely original. Everyone connects arches with elms. One of my students thought of the "Y" and loops for the willow. The duck's leg for pine branches is a Japanese symbol (Kano, I believe).

See if you can find new ones for other trees or better ones for these.

CYPRESS. A flat brush, or one flat with rounded corners, for the foliage; for the branches and twigs a round pointed small brush.

LOMBARDY POPLAR. Quick, dry, vertical strokes. A rigger or thin, round brush is good for the branches. Aim for the zenith.

MAPLE. Elliptical fuzzy strokes with a big brush. Note the relative size of the trunk and branches; also the way the branches are attached and the spherical solid outer shape with dark holes in it.

WILLOW. A dry brush dragged lightly downward. Make the willow weep and drip.

FIR. Arrowheads, painted with dark tube color and almost no water.

OAK. For the branches use angles and arcs, all that the geometry book affords. Add warts. The foliage is best done by patting.

BIRCH. Bark peeled off. Dark triangles at the branch attachments.

CEDAR. Done, for the most part, with one upward stroke of a dry, dark brush. Push it, point first, away from you; the splaying out of the hairs gives the silhouette.

PINE. Short pushes with a dry flat stroke-brush or an oil painter's brush give the needles. Pines are often one-sided as to branches.

ELM. The elm branches do not droop as much in winter as in summer. When full of sap the leaves of an elm weigh down the limbs. Note the lozenge-shaped air-holes between the branches.

APPLE. Nearly always a branch or two sawed off. The trunk usually leans one way or the other. A pear-tree in shape is a composite of the elm and the apple.

PALM. A pointed round brush used dry; the same type of stroke as with the fir-tree.

Observation

All color is relative to the colors surrounding it. In judging what color to paint a thing, do not look at the thing itself but at a neighboring piece of color. If a house is seen against the sky and you are ready to paint the house, fix your eyes on the sky and without focussing them on the house at all, ask yourself what color and value it should have. When determining your sky color, do it while focussing your eyes on the house.

Things as they become more distant should become paler or lighter in value and bluer. An over-emphasis of this usual effect will give better third dimension. The exception to this rule is looking toward the late sun on a misty day when the distant things are warmer than those in the foreground.

A large area of color in landscape is rarely uniform in value or hue. Sky on a cloudless day or on a completely foggy or dull day varies so imperceptibly that it is often painted as a uniform piece. Cut two holes the size of dimes three or four inches apart in a piece of white paper and hold it up before the face; then look with one eye at the sky alternately through one hole and the other. Whether you hold them up and down or from side to side you will be surprised at the difference. Over-emphasize this difference as usual to allow for the fainter indoor illumination of your picture.

English painters have an idea that by turning the head upside down so that one sees the landscape wrong side up one can better judge color. I could never see much difference; but the spectacle of countless artists earnestly standing on their heads all over England has its possibilities. The English watercolorists do get extremely subtle effects in their middle values, and can paint foggy and gray days more sympathetically than artists of any other nation. Looking at things upside down may dissociate the things from their color so that our minds do not pervert our sight. It is true that because we know a house is painted white or that grass is green or sky blue, there is a temptation to see it as white, blue, or green; when it may not be so in relation to its environment.

Outdoors your picture is illuminated with many times the light which shines on it indoors, so that it will look more brilliant in color than it really is. To make it brilliant enough inside, purposely exaggerate all the colors and values. If you see a suggestion of a color in a certain thing, paint it with a considerable strength of that color.

Expression

Listen to as many teachers and painters and read as many books on art as possible, but accept only what is plausible. Don't get under the spell of any one master. Change schools frequently. No one man knows everything. Listen to the moderns with interest, try to name the charlatans among them. Give equal attention to the conservatives; try to name the "old chromos" among them. Don't persuade yourself that you must like a type of work because it is fashionable or because it has won prizes or has been well spoken of by connoisseurs or because some museum has bought it. The judges of art are almost as fallible as yourself. Many talkers and writers on art are more interested in impressing you with their vocabulary or holding their job or attracting public notice than in analyzing the conventions or forces which produce a given type of picture. Many of them are guessing and speculating. Reproduce nature photographically if you wish. If you do it well enough, that is an accomplishment. Interpret nature, if you will; you may do it in terms which will be entirely new. Merely suggest trains of thought to the beholder if you have sufficient power of suggestion. Express yourself if you think others will be interested; probably they won't be, but they may pretend they are. Think in terms of color, or mass, or make pure abstractions. None of these things has yet been well enough done.

But, whatever you do, do it without shame or fear of what any particular friend or critic will think. If you do any one of these things well enough, you will find acceptance and a public, enemies and defenders.

A PARTIAL BIBLIOGRAPHY
OF USEFUL BOOKS FOR
THE WATERCOLORIST

The Technique of Water-Color Painting, L. Richmond, R.O.I., R.B.A., and J. Littlejohns, R.B.A. Sir Isaac Pitman & Sons, Ltd., 1925.

On the Laws of Japanese Painting, Henry P. Bowie. Paul Elder & Co., Publishers, San Francisco.

Figure-Painting in Water Colors, by Contemporary British Artists. The Studio Ltd., 1923.

British Water-Color Painting and Painters of Today, J. Littlejohns, R.B.A., R.B.C., A.R.W.A. Isaac Pitman & Sons, 1931.

Practical Water-color Sketching, E. G. Lutz. Charles Scribner's Sons, 1931.

The Practice of Water-Color Painting, G. L. Baldry. The Macmillan Co., 1911.

The Art of Water-Color Painting, E. Barnard Lintott. Charles Scribner's Sons, 1926.

Color, Cutler & Pepper. Harvard University Press.

Painting and the Personal Equation, Charles H. Woodbury, N.A. Houghton Mifflin Co., 1919.

History of Art, Elie Faure. *Modern Art,* trans. by Walter Pach. Harper & Bros.

The Art Spirit, Robert Henri, compiled by Margery Ryerson. J. B. Lippincott, 1930.

Famous Water-Color Painters (Reproductions), Sargent, Brangwyn, Flint, Blake, etc. The Studio, London.

Water-color Renderings of Venice, North Italy, etc., Pierre Vignal. J. H. Jansen, Cleveland, Ohio.

Architectural Shades and Shadows. Henry McGoodwin. Bates & Guild Co., Boston, 1926.

Due	DUE	Due	DUE
JA30'67			